# HACKERTEEN

# HACKERTEEN ™
## VOLUME 1: INTERNET BLACKOUT
by Marcelo Marques & the Hackerteen Team

Published by O'Reilly Media, Inc., 1005 Gravenstein Highway North, Sebastopol, CA 95472.

O'Reilly books may be purchased for educational, business, or sales promotional use. Online editions are also available for most titles (*safari.oreilly.com*). For more information, contact our corporate/institutional sales department: 800.998.9938 or *corporate@oreilly.com*.

Printing History:

April 2008: First Edition.

ISBN: 978-0-596-51647-5

[F]

# HACKERTEEN

# INTERNET BLACKOUT

### VOLUME 1

## MARCELO MARQUES
## & THE HACKERTEEN TEAM

## O'REILLY®

BEIJING • CAMBRIDGE • FARNHAM • KÖLN • PARIS • SEBASTOPOL • TAIPEI • TOKYO

YAGO IS A COMPUTER WIZARD, BUT SPENDS MOST OF HIS TIME PLAYING GAMES, ON MYSPACE, MSN, ETC.

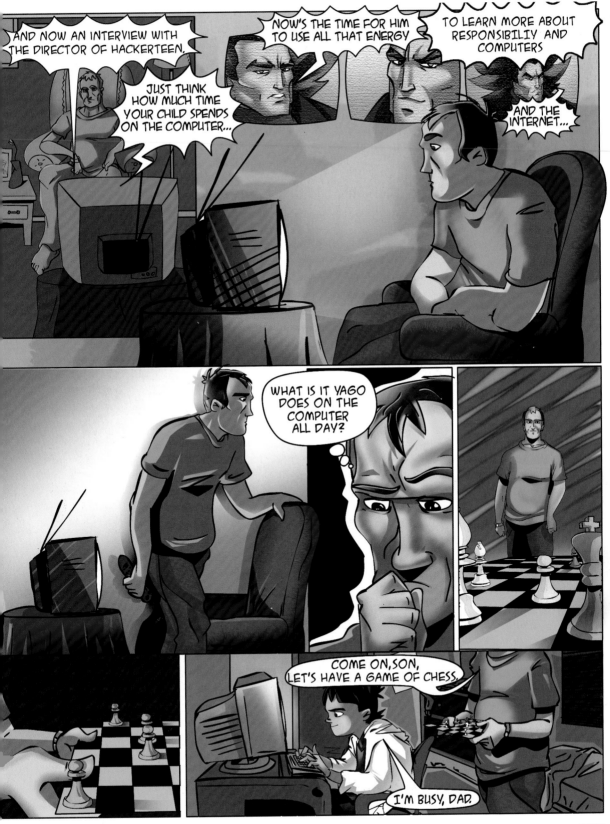

IT'S IN THE BOAT!

I WONDER WHAT A MONK COULD BE TEACHING HERE.

YOU'VE GOT 20 MINUTES TO PROTECT THE SERVERS, STARTING...NOW!

CALCULATE THE IP ADDRESS TO FIND OUT WHICH CAVE TO ENTER. ONE MINUTE!

THE NEXT CLASS IS ABOUT A DDOS ATTACK ON THE DNS SERVERS IN 2000.

I FORGET WHAT DNS STANDS FOR.

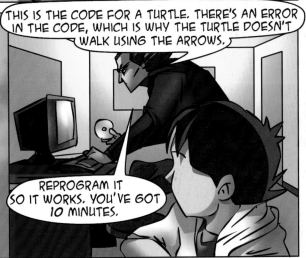

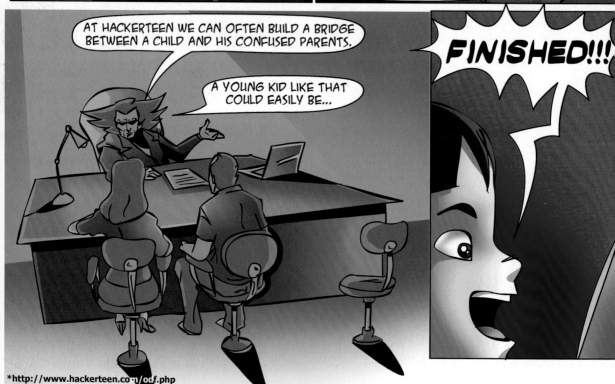

*http://www.hackerteen.com/odf.php

TAKING HACKERTEEN CLASSES...

*http://www.hackerteen.com/ethical_hacker.php

14

"INTRUSION ATTEMPT, BAKERY. VULNERABILITY REGISTER SCAN 216."

SON, THAT COMPUTER OF YOURS IS INFECTED!

INFECTED!

DON'T WORRY, DAD, I'LL GET RID OF THOSE MESSAGES. THEY'RE AUTOMATIC ROBOTS* TRYING TO INVADE UNPROTECTED COMPUTERS. I'M MONITORING THEM 24 HOURS A DAY.

AT THE CASOY RESIDENCE.

YOU'VE GOT TO SEE THIS SKIRT I BOUGHT, IT'S AWESOME!

DIANA, YOU STILL DON'T HAVE A WEBCAM? YOU COULD BE SHOWING ME RIGHT NOW.

OH YEAH, I KEEP FORGETTING. I'LL BUY ONE, I PROMISE.

DAD?

HEY DAD, WHAT ARE YOU DOING?

TRYING TO FIGURE OUT HOW I'M GOING TO COMPETE WITH THIS DAMN SUPERMARKET.

HAVE YOU SEEN THE ENORMOUS BREAD SECTION THEY HAVE IN THERE?

WIKIPE, I NEED A FAVOR. CAN YOU COVER FOR ME AND TAKE MY FORENSIC* SCIENCE CLASS?

YOUR CUSTOMERS ARE CLASSY ENOUGH FOR FRESH BAKED GOODS, BUT EVERYTHING HERE'S IN PLASTIC.

WOULDN'T YOU BE INTERESTED IN SELLING FRESH BREAD?

NO ROOM, NO TIME, NO STAFF... I'D NEED AN OVEN AND THERE'S NO SPACE!

LOOK, I HAVE AN IDEA...

LATER AT THE MALL...

CRASH!!!

I'M SORRY.

IT'S OK...

26

*http://www.hackerteen.com/ballotbox.php

YAGO'S HOME...

DAD, THIS IS THE MANAGER AT THE SUPERMARKET. HE WANTS TO SPEAK TO YOU.

THAT SUPERMARKET? WHAT DOES HE WANT?

YOU'LL SEE, DAD. DON'T WORRY, IT'S GOOD.

TEACHERS AT A HACKERTEEN CLASS...

TODAY'S CLASS IS ABOUT DIGITAL CERTIFICATION.*

I WONDER HOW THIS WORKS. I SHOULD'VE GOTTEN THAT GUY'S NUMBER.

MANUAL

WEBCAM

*http://www.hackerteen.com/digitalcertification.php

SO, IN SUMMARY, DIGITAL CERTIFICATION DEPENDS ON EACH USER REMEMBERING AND SECURING HIS OR HER PRIVATE KEY. YOUR CHALLENGE IS TO STICK TO THESE GOALS UNDER A VARIETY OF SCENARIOS.

OK, GUYS, NOW YOU HAVE **20** MINUTES TO COMPLETE THE CHALLENGE. YOU MAY START.

NOT AGAIN!

WHAT'S UP?

PEOPLE CALLING ME ASKING ME TO DO WEIRD JOBS.

CRIMINALS TRYING TO MAKE MONEY OFF OF OUR KNOWLEDGE.

KNOWLEDGE WE WERE TAUGHT IN ORDER TO DO GOOD THINGS.

YOU'RE GOING TO GET CALLS LIKE THAT ALL THE TIME FROM NOW ON, BECAUSE YOU'RE A BROWN BELT. I DO.

BUT HOW DO THEY KNOW I'M A BROWN BELT NOW?

AT HACKERTEEN'S WEB PAGE.

HACKERIP'S ORDERING A CONFERENCE CALL WITH ALL HACKERTEENS, IN ONE MINUTE IN THE VIP ROOM.

APPLICATIONS ARE NOW OPEN FOR THE XI HACKER CHALLENGE.Z

GREAT.

AWESOME!

COOL.

HACKERTEEN WILL TAKE PART AS USUAL. POWER, YOU'RE RESPONSIBLE FOR PUTTING TOGETHER A TEAM. GET BACK TO ME TOMORROW SO I CAN SIGN US UP. THAT'S ALL FOR NOW.

YOU'RE FROM HACKERTEEN, RIGHT?

MY WIFE HAS BEEN CHEATING ON ME. I'D LIKE YOU TO HELP ME KEEP AN EYE ON HER.

I DON'T DO THAT SORT OF WORK.

I JUST NEED YOU TO CREATE A PROGRAM TO TRACE* ALL HER ONLINE MOVEMENTS. JUST TO FIND OUT WHO IT IS...WE HAVE TWO CHILDREN, PLEASE HELP!

I'M SORRY...

I UNDERSTAND. LOOK, HERE'S MY CARD IN CASE YOU CHANGE YOUR MIND.

Marlon Casoy
phone
11-493-1292

SEE?! I FINALLY GOT MY WEBCAM!

WOW, THE IMAGE IS SO SHARP! WHAT'S THAT NECKLACE YOU'RE WEARING?

SOMETHING I PICKED UP AT THE MALL.

MUCH BETTER CHATTING WITH A WEBCAM.

YEAH. PLUS WHILE I WAS SHOPPING, I RAN INTO A BOY WHO HELPED ME CHOOSE IT. HE WAS CUTE.

I'M PUTTING TOGETHER THE TEAM FOR THE CHALLENGE AND WE NEED SIX MEMBERS. CAN I COUNT ON YOU?

I'M SORRY, POWER, I HAD TO SELL MY PC TO HELP OUT MY DAD.

WHAT A DRAG!

YEAH, THINGS ARE A BIT DIFFICULT AT HOME.

ALL RIGHT, I'LL FIGURE SOMETHING OUT, SEE YOU TOMORROW.

DID HE BITE?

NOT YET, GIVE HIM A COUPLE OF DAYS.

INSIDE AN OFFICE...

LOOK, WE'VE TRIED TO INVADE HACKERIP'S COMPUTER A DOZEN TIMES. IT'S IMPENETRABLE.

ALL RIGHT, FORGET HACKERIP'S COMPUTER. I'VE GOT ANOTHER IDEA. GET ME INFO ON THE LEADING HACKER WHO CONTRIBUTES TO THE OPEN SOURCE DNS CODE.*

HIS NAME IS DNSOLVER.

REMEMBER THE EXPLOIT YOU FOUND IN DNSOLVER'S CODE THAT LETS YOU BRING DOWN A DNS SERVER?

I WANT TO BUY IT.

HONEY, YOU'VE BEEN AT THE COMPUTER FOR AGES, HOW ABOUT GOING OUT FOR DINNER TONIGHT?

DIANA?

OH, NOT TONIGHT, GRANDMA, I NEED TO FINISH THIS.

THE CASOY RESIDENCE.

THAT KID LOOKS FAMILIAR.

IMPIUS? IT CAN'T BE...

BUT I WROTE THAT MYSELF

THEN TELL ME WHAT'S ON THE SIXTH LINE OF THE PROGRAM.

AN IF STATEMENT.

SCROLL THE SCREEN TO THE SIXTH LINE, PLEASE.

```
int retry = 0;
int reprise;
unsigned long *R_Off
char *data;
if (!Buffer_List[ID].da
return -1;
    Offset = (unsigned
```

```
unsigned long *
char *data;
if (!Buffe     ID].data)
return -
R_Of
```

THE WINNING GROUP IS HACKERTEEN!

THE TEAM THAT CHEATED IS BANNED FROM ALL FUTURE HACKER CHALLENGE EVENTS.

ONE DAY, YOU'LL GET A TASTE OF 666.

GUYS, WE SAW UNETHICAL BEHAVIOR IN ACTION TODAY. WHEN WE TAKE PART IN THE TECH PARTY EVENT, I'D LIKE US TO LAUNCH SOMETHING THAT HELPS PREVENT SUCH BEHAVIOR.

HOW ABOUT A BOOKLET AIMED AT YOUNG PEOPLE?

A BOOKLET ABOUT MISUSE OF COMPUTERS AND THE INTERNET?

WHAT SORT OF BOOKLET?

HOW ABOUT A PDF* SHOWING THE PROS AND CONS OF SOME OF THE TECHNOLOGIES YOUNG PEOPLE USE?

WHAT TECHNOLOGIES?

WELL, YOU TELL ME

WHAT DO YOUNG PEOPLE USE? YAGO, I WANT YOU TO BE IN CHARGE OF PUTTING THIS BOOKLET TOGETHER, ALL RIGHT?

*http://www.hackerteen.com/fileextensions.php

THIS IS THE BALLOT BOX'S CODE, BUT YOU NEED THE ACTUAL BOX TO FIND OUT HOW IT WORKS.

ALAN, THE BOX WILL BE PRESENTED LIVE AT THE TECH PARTY EVENT. WE'LL SEE IT THERE. HACKERTEEN WILL HAVE A BOOTH.

WHAT ELSE DO YOU WANT ME TO DO?

TRY TO FIND OUT WHAT IMPIUS HAS BEEN UP TO LATELY.

AT ALAN'S HOUSE...

TAKE ME TO THE BANK.

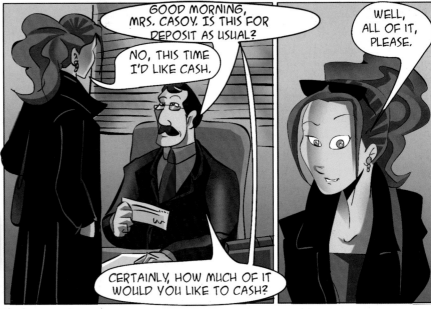

GOOD MORNING, MRS. CASOY. IS THIS FOR DEPOSIT AS USUAL?

NO, THIS TIME I'D LIKE CASH.

WELL, ALL OF IT, PLEASE.

CERTAINLY, HOW MUCH OF IT WOULD YOU LIKE TO CASH?

57

IT'S A LOT OF MONEY, ARE YOU SURE?

YES, THANK YOU.

AMAZON PARK

ATHENA

ALSO, I'M GIVING THE WHOLE TEAM TICKETS TO SEE THE FIRST NIGHT OF THE BLUE SCREEN PLAY.

WILL WE GET TO MEET A LOT OF GREAT HACKERS THERE?

I EXPECT SO.

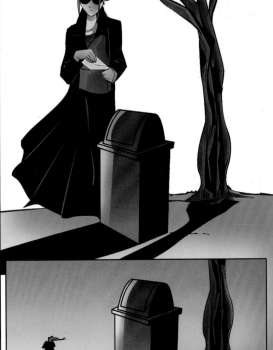

HACKERTEEN

YES, YES, I'M CHARGING $ 1500.

HACKERTEEN

click

SELLING SOMETHING?

YEAH, MY NINTENDO.

SEE YOU AT THE THEATER.

WE GOT CUT OFF. WHAT'S THE JOB?

I JUST NEED TO FIND OUT WHAT A PROGRAM ON MY COMPUTER DOES.

IS THAT ALL?

THAT'S IT.

ALL RIGHT, I'LL DO IT. EMAIL THE PROGRAM TO ME.

I'D RATHER DELIVER IT PERSONALLY.

MEET ME IN HALF AN HOUR IN AMAZON PARK. I'LL NEED HALF UP FRONT.

I'M IN TROUBLE NO

SURPRISE!

SURPRISE!

SURPRISE!

SURPRISE!

SURPRISE!

SURPRISE!

YOU DESERVE AND NEED THIS MUCH MORE THAN WE DO.

A TOAST TO YAGO, AND TO HACKERTEEN. WE'VE HAD SOME FINANCIAL DIFFICULTIES RECENTLY, BUT THANKS TO ALL THE OVERTIME WORK YOU'VE BEEN GIVING HIM, WE'VE BEEN ALL RIGHT.

ALL RIGHT, EVERYONE, LET'S GO TO THE THEATER.

GUYS, TOMORROW WE START WORK ON THE BOOKLET. WE'LL MEET AT HACKERTEEN TO GET A MOVE ON IT.

I PROPOSE THE NAME "VIRTUAL DIALOG" FOR THE BOOKLET.

Calling...
DNSolver

NO ANSWER...

HONEY, WHAT'S WRONG, WHAT IS IT?

GRANDMA, THAT $10,000 WASN'T FOR A COURSE.

I'M BEING BLACKMAILED, IT'S TOO AWFUL. NOW THEY WANT $100,000.

AT HOME...

SOME HOURS LATER...

WHO CAN THAT BE SO LATE?

OF COURSE, JUST A MINUTE.

NO, THERE'S NOTHING WRITTEN ON THE BACK.

"GIVE ME ANOTHER $100,000 OR I'LL PUBLISH ALL THE VIDEOS ON THE INTERNET. TOMORROW, SAME PLACE."

FRED, I'M BEING BLACKMAILED! I WANT YOU TO FIND THE TOP EXPERT IN THE CITY ON INTERNET CRIME, GET THESE CROOKS, AND PUT THEM BEHIND BARS!

AT HOME, HACKERIP STUDIES THE BALLOT BOX CODES MORE CLOSELY.

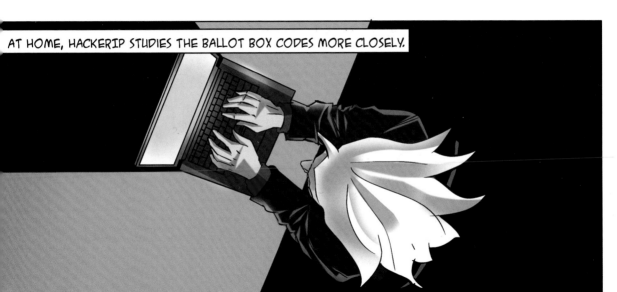

NO ANSWER...

I'LL LEAVE A MESSAGE...

MR. CASOY, I'M ON MY WAY TO YOUR PLACE. THEY'VE FOUND OUT YOU'RE TRACING YOUR WIFE. I HAVEN'T UNDERSTOOD EXACTLY WHAT'S GOING ON. ANYWAY, DON'T LET ON THAT YOU RECOGNIZE ME.

Hacker IP,
Alan has been arrested and accused of an illicit investigation against the President. Sufficient evidence was found on his computer to incriminate him. With this Anti-Hacker Law in force, Alan is in jail, with a hearing in a few days.

I'M SORRY, SIR, BUT NO VISITORS ARE ALLOWED.

WE CAN'T HELP OUR FRIENDS DNSOLVER AND ALAN RIGHT NOW, BUT WE HAVE A CHANCE AT THE DEBATE. LET ME SEE THE BOOKLET FOR TOMORROW.

WELL, I THINK THE SECTION ON SOCIAL NETWORKS NEEDS IMPROVING BUT OTHERWISE IT SEEMS FINE.

YAGO, FINISH IT SO WE CAN LAUNCH IT ON THE HACKERTEEN WEBSITE RIGHT BEFORE THE ANNOUNCEMENT AT THE FAIR TOMORROW.

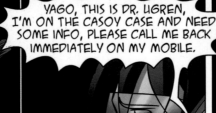

HI UGREN. I FORGOT TO PASS ON YOUR QUESTION, BUT YOU CAN CALL YAGO DIRECTLY, HE HAS ALL THE DETAILS.

I'LL GIVE YOU HIS NUMBER.

1 voice message!

YAGO, THIS IS DR. UGREN, I'M ON THE CASOY CASE AND NEED SOME INFO, PLEASE CALL ME BACK IMMEDIATELY ON MY MOBILE.

82

BUT HOW CAN YOU BE SURE THE CODE THAT WAS AUDITED AND APPROVED IS THE SAME THAT WILL BE USED IN THE FINAL BALLOT BOX?

THE COMPANY WOULD NEVER RISK ITS REPUTATION THAT WAY.

R.A.

NOT SO FAR AWAY...

DNSOLVER COULD GO TO JAIL FOR UP TO 3 YEARS.

WE'VE FOLLOWED ALL NORMS AND STANDARDS OF THE ANTI-HACKER LAW.

HOW CAN YOU GUARANTEE VOTERS' PRIVACY?

HAVEN'T YOU READ THE LAW? ALL SUCH MATTERS ARE GUARANTEED.

BUT THIS DOESN'T PROTECT CITIZENS! IT LEAVES THEM HIGHLY VULNERABLE! YOU'RE GOING TO COLLECT SAMPLES OF HUMAN DNA FOR ALL USERS, WHICH COULD BE USED FOR COMMERCIAL OR POLITICAL PURPOSES.

SEE YOU AT THE DEBATE IN 15 MINUTES, SENATOR!

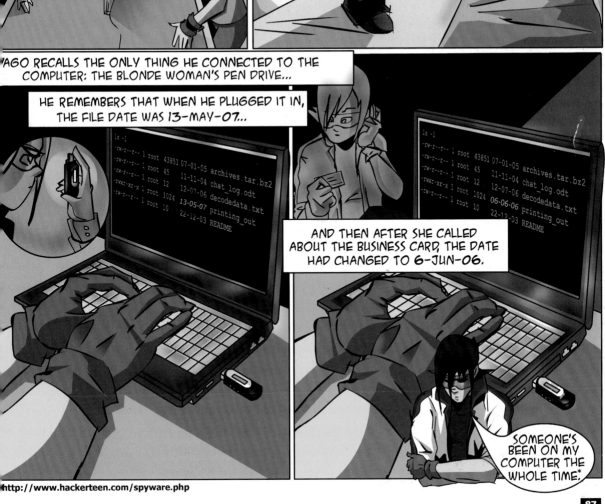

THE FIGHT TO SAVE THE INTERNET BEGINS...

SOMEONE ENHANCES THE CELNETY GAME TO REFLECT THE CURRENT CRISIS WITH 12 MILLION INFECTED SYSTEMS.

FREE-SOFTWARE* PROGRAMMERS MAKE A TEST ENVIRONMENT FOR CELL PHONES THAT SIMULATES THE 13 DNS SERVERS.

You can test the DNS cure on the CELNETY Game.

RESEARCHERS WORK DAY AND NIGHT TO ASSEMBLE A SAFETY NET THAT WOULD PREVENT THE COMPUTERS WITH THE ETHICS BOOKLET ON THEM FROM CARRYING OUT THE ATTACK, BUT THE ATTACK CODE CONTAINS OVER 10 MILLION LINES.

I DOUBT THAT IT'LL BE POSSIBLE TO DEBUG 10 MILLION LINES IN SUCH A SHORT TIME.

STOCK EXCHANGES START TO FALL.

*http://www.hackerteen.com/free_software.php

A WEB 2.0* SITE IS LAUNCHED FOR HACKERS AROUND THE PLANET TO COLLABORATE ON FINDING A DEFENSE.

BUT SOON, A HACKER POSTS A MESSAGE ARGUING THAT THE 10 MILLION LINES ARE A RED HERRING TO MAKE EVERYONE WASTE THEIR TIME WHILE THE INTERNET GRINDS TO A HALT.

THE POSTER'S SUGGESTION IS TO FIX THE VULNERABILITY PRESENT IN THE DNS, ALLOWING THE ATTACK TO TAKE PLACE BUT NOT ALLOWING IT TO HAVE THE INTENDED EFFECT.

THE WORLD'S NEWS NETWORKS REPORT THE LAUNCH OF THIS NEW SITE.

WEB 2.0 Solution

The Internet Blackout!

MORE AND MORE HACKERS HEAR ABOUT IT, STOP WHAT THEY'RE DOING, AND VISIT THE PAGE.

WITH THE WEB 2.0 SITE OFFERING BETTER ACCESS TO THE OPEN SOURCE DNS CODE, THOUSANDS OF HACKERS OF EVERY RACE, SEX, AND ETHNIC GROUP AROUND THE WORLD COLLABORATE TO NEUTRALIZE THE ATTACK.

GRADUALLY A SOLUTION STARTS TO COME TOGETHER. THE WORLD'S MOST FAMOUS HACKERS TAKE COMMAND OF THE MOVEMENT.

WITH EACH CORRECTION, THEY TEST IT AND SHARE IT WORLDWIDE.

HACKERTEEN STUDENTS, WITHOUT YAGO, MEET DAILY TO PUT THEIR SKILLS INTO THE WORLDWIDE EFFORT.

Send

File

*http://www.hackerteen.com/web20.php

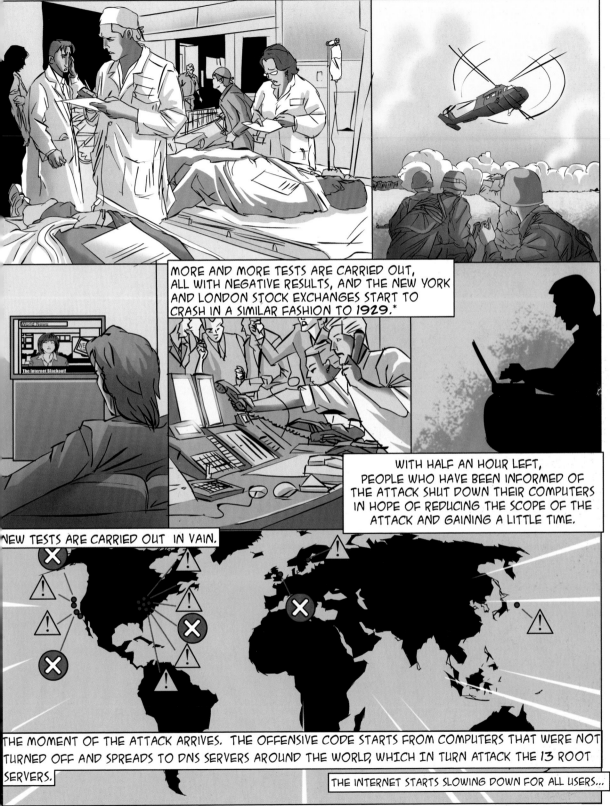

MORE AND MORE TESTS ARE CARRIED OUT, ALL WITH NEGATIVE RESULTS, AND THE NEW YORK AND LONDON STOCK EXCHANGES START TO CRASH IN A SIMILAR FASHION TO 1929.*

WITH HALF AN HOUR LEFT, PEOPLE WHO HAVE BEEN INFORMED OF THE ATTACK SHUT DOWN THEIR COMPUTERS IN HOPE OF REDUCING THE SCOPE OF THE ATTACK AND GAINING A LITTLE TIME.

NEW TESTS ARE CARRIED OUT IN VAIN.

THE MOMENT OF THE ATTACK ARRIVES. THE OFFENSIVE CODE STARTS FROM COMPUTERS THAT WERE NOT TURNED OFF AND SPREADS TO DNS SERVERS AROUND THE WORLD, WHICH IN TURN ATTACK THE 13 ROOT SERVERS.

THE INTERNET STARTS SLOWING DOWN FOR ALL USERS...

*http://www.hackerteen.com/1929.php

SUDDENLY, A NEW TEST IN AN ANONYMOUS CHAT ROOM SUCCEEDS IN RESISTING THE ATTACK CODE. NEWS OF THE BREAKTHROUGH SPREADS AROUND THE GLOBE.

New hope for the Internet Blackout!

THE 13 ROOT SERVERS LOAD THE CORRECTION. ALTHOUGH THE ATTACK CONTINUES, THE INTERNET STARTS TO RECOVER ITS FORMER SPEED.

DNS ADMINISTRATORS RECONFIGURE THEIR TIME-TO-LIVE INTERVALS SO THAT CORRECTED DNS UPDATES SPREAD QUICKLY.

20 MINUTES LATER, THE ANONYMOUS CHATTER WHO POSTED THE FIX SIGNS OFF WITH THE WORDS: "MY KNOWLEDGE REPAID YOUR TRUST."

My knowledge repaid your trust

MOST WHO SEE THE MESSAGE ARE SIMPLY PUZZLED...

BUT HACKERIP HEARS THE INFORMATION COMING FROM A TV AT THE END OF THE HALL, AND GETS THE MESSAGE.

YAGO'S NOT GUILTY... YAGO'S NOT GUILTY.

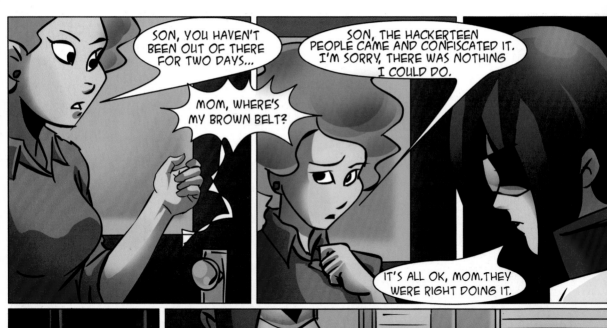

TO BE CONTINUED IN HACKERTEEN VOLUME 2!

STAY TUNED FOR
VOLUME 2...

IN THE NEXT HACKERTEEN
ADVENTURE, YAGO LEAVES
HOME AND DISCOVERS HOW
MUCH FREEDOM HE GAINS
FROM HIS KNOWLEDGE OF
HACKING, COMPUTERS, AND
TECHNOLOGY.

BUT BACK AT HOME, THE
SENATOR AND RESULTS
ASSURANCE CORP. ARE STILL
USING TECHNOLOGY FOR
SINISTER PURPOSES. THEIR
PLAN IS TO GAIN CONTROL
OF EVERY WORLD CITIZEN'S
PERSONAL INFORMATION.
WILL YAGO BE ABLE TO
STOP THEM IN TIME?

# CREDITS

MARCELO MARQUES (author) is a graduate of FASP (Brazil) in business administration, with further degrees in business from the Getulio Vargas Foundation and in marketing from Trevisan. He currently provides IT-related services to a number of multinational companies. In 2001, he developed a business plan and, with three partners, founded 4Linux. The company launched the innovative Hackerteen project, where Marcelo teaches entrepreneurship and marketing. He then assumed the presidency of LPI-Brasil, created entertaining talks on open source software and Linux, and wrote the comedy play *Blue Screen*. Together with a great group (the Hackerteen Team), he created the fantasy content of *Hackerteen*. Currently he serves as Director of Strategy and Marketing at 4Linux and Hackerteen.

HACKERTEEN TEAM (contributors) without whom this graphic novel could never have taken form.

HUGO MOSS (story supervisor) lives in Rio de Janeiro, and provides services to most Brazilian film production companies, whether as screenwriter, consultant, specialist translator, or through other creative work. He holds regular workshops, is the director of several shorts and documentaries, and is a permanent collaborator at the NGO Associação Thalamus (*http://www.thalamus.org.br*).

JOÃO FELIPE MUNHOZ (artist) is a self-taught illustrator, comic book writer, and cartoonist, who received basic training in technical drafting for advertising purposes at the Mario de Andrade School. In 1998 he moved into the publishing business, creating illustrations for children's books and a wide array of periodicals. Since he began his career as a cartoonist in 2006, he has been publishing his work in a daily tabloid with a circulation of 200,000.

FABIO PONTES RAMON FELIN (colorist) is creator of the Japan Sunset group. For the past 12 years he's been a manga artist and teaching others manga techniques. His art appears in various places, including newspapers, magazines, and illustrations.

RAFAEL KIRSCHNER (colorist) is a penciler, illustrator, colorist, and inker. Since 2000, he's been teaching techniques of all drawing styles, including manga. His work can be seen in comics of all genres and newspapers.

RICARDO BOMFIM (colorist) has worked as a colorist, penciler, and inker for nine years. His work has appeared in various magazines, illustrations, and newspapers.

Publication of this book was made possible by many people at O'Reilly Media, including Andy Oram (editor), Isabel Kunkle and Marlowe Shaeffer (project management), Sarah Schneider (proofreader), Ron Bilodeau (interior design), Karen Montgomery (cover design), and Sue Willing (manufacturing).

HACKERTEEN (*www.hackerteen.com*) is an educational project that teaches adolescents about computer network security, entrepreneurship on the Internet, and hacker ethics. Its innovative methods include challenges, games, RPGs, Linux, and comics.

Three growing social problems provided the motivation for establishing Hackerteen:

1. Excessive time spent by young people surfing and playing computer games on the Internet

2. Young people committing digital crimes on the Internet or being blackmailed

3. A growing lack of professionals who work with networks and computer security

Hackerteen graduates have taken jobs in the computer industry and are teaching their skills to others. Hackerteen is internationally recognized and has won awards for its creative work.